Looking After Your Pet

Your Guinea Pig

Written by
Rebecca Phillips-Bartlett

KidHaven
PUBLISHING

Published in 2026 by
KidHaven Publishing, an Imprint of
Greenhaven Publishing, LLC
2544 Clinton St., Buffalo, NY 14224

Written by: Rebecca Phillips-Bartlett
Edited by: E.C. Andrews
Designed by: Amelia Harris

Cataloging-in-Publication Data
Names: Phillips-Bartlett, Rebecca.
Title: Your Guinea Pig / Rebecca Phillips-Bartlett.
Description: Buffalo, NY : Kidhaven Publishing, 2026. | Series: Looking after your pet | Includes index and glossary
Identifiers: ISBN 9781534550636 (pbk) | ISBN 9781534550643 (library bound) | ISBN 9781534550650 (ebook)
Subjects: LCSH: Guinea pigs--Juvenile Literature | Pets—Juvenile Literature
Classification: LCC SF459.G9 P45 2026 | DDC 636.93592 --dc25

Manufactured in the United States of America

CPSIA compliance information: Batch #CSKH26
For further information contact Greenhaven Publishing LLC at 1-844-317-7404.

Please visit our website, www.greenhavenpublishing.com.
For a free color catalog of all our high-quality books, call toll free 1-844-317-7404 or fax 1-844-317-7405.

Find us on

Image Credits

Images are courtesy of Shutterstock.com. With thanks to Getty Images, Thinkstock Photo, and iStockphoto. Cover – Artishok, Dev_Maryna, Happy monkey. Recurring Images – Victoria Nevzorova, Vladislav Lyutovm, Irina Loongu. 2–3 – Miroslav Hlavko. 4–5 – New Africa, Pixel-Shot. 6–7 – Rita_Kochmarjova, New Africa. 8–9 – Pasindhu sandeepa, Hinzefoto. 10–11 – Annabell Gsoedl, MarcoFood, Millie21, Greens and Blues, GreenSkyStudio. 12–13 – vovan, Dev_Maryna. 14–15 – Jackson Stock Photography, PHOTO FUN, mariesacha. 16–17 – SrideeStudio, Pressmaster, Monkey Business Images. 18–19 – Naomi Marcin, Tetiana Dickens. 20–21 – cynoclub, Lost_in_the_Midwest, trabantos. 22–23 – LevkovskayaAleksandra, Pixel-Shot.

Contents

Words that look like this can be found in the glossary on page 24.

A Perfect Pet

Whether they are big or small, pets become part of the family! Guinea pigs are adorable, chatty rodents. They make perfect pets for many people. However, having a fluffy family member is a big responsibility.

Do you have a pet guinea pig? Or are you thinking about getting one? Either way, this guide is full of tips to teach you how to care for your perfect pet.

Getting Guinea Pigs

You can get guinea pigs from rescue centers, pet shops, and breeders.

Guinea pigs like living with other guinea pigs. They will get lonely on their own. If you are getting a guinea pig, you should get at least two so they can live together.

Before you get guinea pigs, think about:

- How much space your guinea pigs need
- How much it costs to look after pets, including food, toys, and vet care
- How much time you have to spend with your new friends

Your Guinea Pigs' Place

In some countries, guinea pigs are happiest outside. In other places, they are safest inside.

Guinea pigs need plenty of space so they can run and jump around. Your guinea pigs' home should be very secure so that they are safe and cannot get out.

Your guinea pigs' home should have plenty of bedding. This will help them stay warm and give them somewhere to hide. Guinea pigs only sleep in short naps. They are awake for around 20 hours a day.

Guinea pigs need plenty of toys.

Diet

Guinea pigs mostly eat hay and fresh grass. They also need specially made guinea pig pellets with vitamin C. Leafy greens, such as broccoli and kale, are healthy guinea pig snacks.

Guinea pigs should have some food and water available all the time.

Guinea pigs can eat some fruits and vegetables, such as apples and carrots. Guinea pigs should never eat citrus fruits or iceberg lettuce. Some plants, such as buttercups, can make guinea pigs very sick.

Before feeding your guinea pigs, ask a grown-up to check what they can eat.

Playtime

Guinea pigs need to be able to play with other guinea pigs. Some guinea pigs love to play with humans too. Playing with your guinea pigs every day will help them get plenty of exercise.

Always be gentle so you do not scare your fluffy friends!

Guinea pigs love to play all day and night. They need enough toys to keep them busy when you cannot play. Their toys should be wooden, not plastic, so they can chew on them safely.

Keeping Clean

Just like you keep your bedroom clean, it is important to keep your guinea pigs' space clean. Their home should be cleaned every week. You will need to clean out poop every day.

When you clean the cage, leave some old bedding inside so it still smells like home.

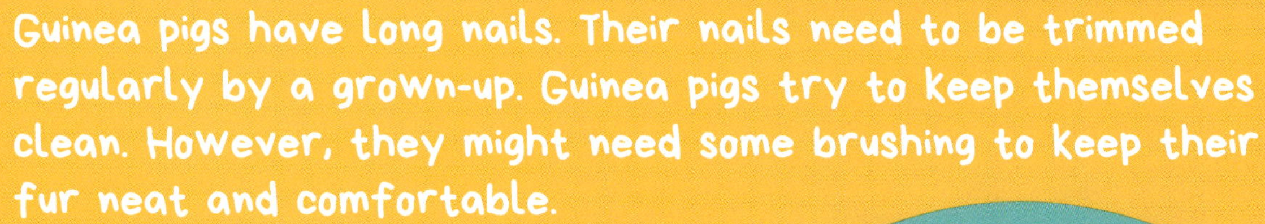

Guinea pigs have long nails. Their nails need to be trimmed regularly by a grown-up. Guinea pigs try to keep themselves clean. However, they might need some brushing to keep their fur neat and comfortable.

Long-haired guinea pigs need brushing each week.

The Vet

The vet is like a doctor for your pet.

Not all vets can look after guinea pigs. Before getting guinea pigs, check whether your vet can care for them. Your guinea pigs will need to visit the vet for a check-up every year.

Just like humans, animals can get sick. If you notice that one of your guinea pigs is acting strangely, such as not eating or hiding more than usual, tell a grown-up.

Your guinea pig will go to the vet in a carrier.

Growing Up

Like all living things, guinea pigs change throughout their lives. Baby guinea pigs are called pups. Pups grow very quickly. Young guinea pigs spend a lot of time playing and exploring.

Guinea pigs become adults at around six months. Some adult guinea pigs become less active. You might need to encourage them to exercise. At five years old, guinea pigs become seniors. Seniors might need special food.

Guinea pigs normally live for five to seven years.

Fantastic Guinea Pig Facts

Guinea pigs love to show their feelings! Happy guinea pigs are known for jumping up high and turning in the air. This is called popcorning.

Guinea pigs come from the Andes Mountains in South America.

In the wild, guinea pigs live in groups called herds.

Just like pigs, a male guinea pig is called a boar. A female guinea pig is called a sow.

Guinea pigs have odd toes. They have four toes on their front feet. However, they only have three toes on their back feet.

An Amazing Owner

Learning the basics of guinea pig care is the first step to becoming an amazing owner. You now know lots about caring for your fluffy friends. However, there is still a lot more to learn.

You and a grown-up will have lots of big decisions to make before getting your guinea pigs. Where will they live? Who will feed them and clean their home?

Are you ready to become an amazing guinea pig owner?

Glossary

breeders people who bring animals together to make babies that they can sell

responsibility being in charge of doing something; doing the things that are supposed to be done

rodents mammals, such as rats, mice, and squirrels, that have long front teeth which grow throughout their whole lives

secure safely fixed so it cannot become loose

vitamin C a substance that humans and some animals do not make that helps protect the body and is needed to build bones, blood vessels, and more

Index